The
Soul
of Man

EDWARD J. LEE

ISBN: 1490946772
ISBN-13: 9781490946771

DEDICATION

This book is dedicated to those who have been struggling for years and looking for answers. To my family, loved ones who have always been there for me and supported me through the ups and downs of life, this is for you. I pray that this book reveals the truth and knowledge of God's power in your life and causes you to be victorious in your mind, spirit, and soul. I confess that I don't have all of the answers of life, but I know a God who does. I truly love you all.

ACKNOWLEDGEMENTS

First, I would like to thank God, especially the person of the Holy Spirit, for giving me the insight and revelation to write and share this with everyone.

I've been putting this book together for several years, writing and then stepping away because it seemed too challenging a subject to tackle when combining information from the soul realm and having a spiritual spin on the subject. I was persistent, and now I'm glad I can say it's finally done, thank you Jesus.

Justin, my oldest son, thanks for letting me spend quality time writing in the comfort of your home; it helped to turn the corner and to put a lot of things in place.

Joshua, my youngest son, thank you for lifting me up in prayer while I was writing, and for being a positive role model for all to see, including myself. I'm very proud of you.

INTRODUCTION

Let's go back to the beginning when God created man. He wanted man to be like Him, able to think for himself and to make decisions based on his own free will. **Gen 2:7 — And Lord God formed man of the dust of the ground, and breathed into his nostrils the breath of life; and man became a living soul.**

It was at this time that Adam had the ability to make decisions influenced by his emotions and mind, because he was completely pure. The only real emotion Adam experienced was agape love — that is, until Eve was presented to him. It was then that man was flooded with a host of other emotions, although they had been in him when he was created.

We must establish that the spirit, soul and body have been put together by God **(I Thessalonians 5:22 and 23 — Abstain from all appearance of evil. And the very God of peace sanctify you wholly; and I pray God your whole spirit and soul and body be preserved blameless unto the coming of our Lord**

Jesus Christ), and that he wants each of those pieces to be sanctified. We now need to break those down to see how these three separate components work.

When people are born again, they receive a new spirit. This spirit always wants to do the correct thing because it is in direct contact with God. The body is neutral, like soil: whatever you put in it will come out. If you plant an apple seed, you will get an apple tree; the same with any seed, the soil will produce whatever is put into it. The body does not have any decision-making process; it only does what it is told.

The primary contributing factor is the soul. Now let's look at what comprises this unique piece of our makeup. The soul contains three separate components:

1) Mind or intellect: some call this the thinker.
2) Emotions: this is called the feeler.
3) Will: this is the chooser, or the part of the soul that makes decisions.

Only two of these components actually figure into the equation, which helps the soul to decide — those would be the mind and the emotions. Now the mind is a pretty awesome piece of equipment, and it is even said that we use only 10% to make decisions. Someone using 15% is considered a genius. What would it be like to use, say, 25% or 50%, or let's think big, let's say 100% of our brainpower?

Now this causes somewhat of a problem.

When we accept Christ as our Savior, we get a new spirit. **II Corinthians 5:17** says **Therefore, if any man be in Christ, he is a new creature; old things are passed away; behold all things have become new.** But we have the same mind/intellect and our emotions are still intact. Unfortunately, we find ourselves making a decision based on our past and not on this new creature that has ever existed before.

And here lies our problem.

Chapter 1

* * *

The Mind

The Bible tells us in **Romans 12:2, "And be not conformed to this world: but by ye transformed by the renewing of our mind, that ye may prove what is that good, and acceptable, and perfect will of God."** But that process takes time. How do we make future decisions based on past information? And not just any decision, but one that will glorify God to the fullest and put us in divine alignment with the path that God wants to take us, one that would propel us into our destiny.

All our present habits, mannerisms and thought patterns are the results of past "programming" from parents, teachers, peers, co-workers, television, and a variety of sources. This programming is often referred to as "old tapes," since our minds retain everything. Some old tapes are good. We may be programmed to stop at a red light, or brush our teeth every day, say thank you when appropriate and act according to certain social standards. We accept these tapes without thinking about them, but we also accept other tapes such as "I have my father's temper, "or "I'm lousy with math, or you make me sick or other negative confessions that come out of our mouths on a regular basis.

When the subconscious mind is full of negative tapes, it's virtually impossible to stay in a positive frame of mind unless those tapes are changed. We must find a way to once and for all remove the triggers that throw us back into the process that has us play those old tapes. **Psalm 6:4 — Return, O Lord, deliver my soul; oh save me for thy mercies' sake.**

Let's look at this in several different parts to analyze how the soul works.

First let's examine the mind, but I want to look at this a little differently. Let's look at what I call the *real* mind of a person, which is the heart. It's important because the mind as we know it can deceive us, but the heart shows the real intent and behavior of a person. But just as there is what I call the real mind, there is another mind. Let's put it this way: there's a subconscious mind that you use on a daily basis for behaviors you have already been trained by time and circumstance to know what to do and not do. For example, if you come to a red light, you already know that you should stop. The Bible tells us in **Proverbs 23:7 (a), for as he thinketh in his heart, so is he**. So the heart of a man determines what he's really thinking, and it will come out in his actions.

In addition to the individual mind, there also exist "collective" minds. When a group of individual minds believe the same theme along with its concepts, they will fight anyone or any group that doesn't agree. Fighting comes in many forms. It might be physical, and lead to wars which we have witnessed since the earth began. Gang violence is rampant in the United States and throughout the world. I have never known a time when there was peace on earth, because there is an ongoing theme involving killing those who disagree with the collective mindset that has an alleged pledge to it. Another form of fighting is seen in the different Christian denominations. Baptism is a great event, but one collective mind believes that if you are not baptized in Jesus's name but in the name of the Father, Son, and Holy Ghost, you are not a Christian. In an attempt to be accepted and please all Christians, my friend got baptized twice — once in Jesus's name and once in the name of the Father, Son, and Holy Ghost.

How does a person think or utilize his mind/intellect or thinker? One large piece of this puzzle is this thing called imagination. It's a pretty large chunk because we see things in our mind in pictures. If I were to say "There is a small red dog sitting on the porch of a bright yellow house," your mind would construct the image. Red dog on yellow porch. The same holds true with your imagination, especially when there are no constraints or boundaries.

The mind creates and stores records of everything that happens to us.

Since the subconscious mind is our driving force, we do what our subconscious believes. And since it will believe anything it is told, we can reprogram it if we bypass the conscious mind and substitute new constructive ideas for the existing negative ones. For example, David replaced fear with courage when he was confronted by the lion and the bear when they were trying to steal his sheep from the herd.

There is a basic law of the mind at work here: whenever your conscious mind is in conflict, your subconscious mind invariably wins. This is called the law of conflict. It can also be stated like this: whenever imagination and logic are in conflict, imagination usually wins.

Let's look at two examples of this through the Word. The first is negative and the second is a positive look at how we think.

James 1:8 — a double-minded man is unstable in all his ways. James was stating that if you try to think in too many different directions (and ultimately only one will be the best one), because there is a conflict you will sway back and forth in your thinking and your decisions. This leads to unstable decisions and will result in unstable results. One minute you're heading in one direction and the next you're going the opposite way. This type of behavior drives those who are committed to follow you crazy.

I Chronicles 12 — This chapter tells the story of David's mighty men of valor who were set in their hearts to make David king. Experts in war, they could use all instruments of war and were able to keep rank, and were disciplined. One description is that they came with a perfect heart. They were not double-minded but ready and able to fight for what they believed and what they imagined, and they could see in their minds that David would be king over all Israel.

People usually try to change their habits through willpower and/or self-discipline. While they may convince themselves of the logical course of action, they still imagine themselves doing what they really desire to do. This is why I say that the heart of a person is the real person. For example, smokers trying to quit still imagine the taste or smell of cigarettes, and dieters imagine how good junk food would taste and then wonder why they backslide into old habits.

Proverbs 20:11 — Even a child is known by his doings, whether his work be pure, and whether it be right. Proverbs tells us that we are known by our doings and not our sayings. The real you will eventually come to the forefront. We all talk a good game and some are better at it than others, but our work will be proven by what we *do* right or wrong. Your works will speak for themselves.

I want to talk about how we formulate things in our minds, using our imaginations. Imagination is the language for the mind and it always seems to win over willpower. For example, a person afraid of the dark could be reacting to something being imagined.

The Bible tells us to cast down every evil imagination and every high thing that exalts itself against the knowledge of God: **II Corinthians 10:5 – Casting down imaginations, and every high thing that exalteth itself against the knowledge of God, and bringing into captivity every thought to the obedience of Christ.** We can now see the power of our imaginations.

Imagination is a great thing. It's how we come up with witty inventions, and how the driver of revelation knowledge flows through us. It's the seed of an evil imagination that gets us in trouble, particularly when the mind can't determine good or evil. It will do everything to bring it to pass.

Genesis 11:1-8 says, And the whole earth was of one language, and of one speech.

²And it came to pass, as they journeyed from the east, that they found a plain in the land of Shinar; and they dwelt there.

³And they said one to another, Go to, let us make brick, and burn them thoroughly. And they had brick for stone, and slime had they for mortar.

⁴And they said, Go to, let us build us a city and a tower, whose top *may reach* unto heaven; and let us make us a name, lest we be scattered abroad upon the face of the whole earth.

⁵And the LORD came down to see the city and the tower, which the children of men builded.

⁶And the LORD said, Behold, the people *is* one, and they have all one language; and this they begin to do: and now nothing will be restrained from them, which they have imagined to do.

⁷Go to, let us go down, and there confound their language, that they may not understand one another's speech.

⁸So the LORD scattered them abroad from thence upon the face of all the earth: and they left off to build the city.

We can see that in verse six, there was nothing impossible to them when they had imagined themselves doing it. This can be positive or negative, but nothing was impossible.

So now we see that new habits must replace our old habits. Some habits are easy to eliminate; others are held tightly by the mind.

Imagination usually wins out over logic, and since this is true, we must be motivated to change at a heart level in order to change a habit permanently. This programming can either propel us into success against all odds, or keep us from it in spite of our best efforts. In order to succeed, then, it becomes vitally important to learn how to gain and maintain control of our own programming.

Once your subconscious mind learns something it does not like to change, and the more you try to force the change, the greater the resistance. Logic works with the conscious mind, but not often with the subconscious. For example, 97% of people who pay money to lose weight find it again in fewer than two years. In other words, diets work on the body but not the mind; and unless the subconscious is changed, willpower is only temporary.

We must renew our minds through the Word of God. **Romans 12:2 — And be not conformed to this world: but be ye transformed by the renewing of your mind, that ye may prove what is that good, and acceptable, and perfect, will of God.**

I believe that this is the most challenging but most rewarding thing you can and should do as a Christian, not only when you give your heart to God but throughout your Christian life.

Psalm 51:10 - Create in me a clean heart, O God; and renew a right spirit within me. This was David's request to the Lord. He knew that his heart was not in the right place and that change was necessary for him to continue to be king and lead people in the right direction.

The mind can either be your master or your servant. The mind does not think, it merely reacts to the pictures it is presented. Remember, imagination is the language for the mind.

Nature dislikes a vacuum or empty space, so new habits must replace old ones. Some habits are easy to eliminate; others are held tenaciously by the subconscious.

RULES OF THE MIND

#1: Every thought or idea causes a physical reaction.

Your thoughts can affect all the functions of your body. *Worry* thoughts trigger changes in the stomach that in time can lead to ulcers. *Anger* thoughts stimulate your adrenal glands and the increased adrenaline in the blood stream causes many bodily changes. *Anxiety* and *fear* thoughts affect your pulse rate. There was once a show on television called Fear Factor where contestants won large sums of money by overcoming certain fear challenges that were presented to them. Sometimes just the mere thought of things can send chills or uneasy feelings through your physical body. Just recently I was on the patio of a hotel several floors above the ground and the thought of falling off made me feel uneasy. I'm not really afraid of heights, but the thought drove me to feel that way.

#2: What's expected tends to be realized.

This is also called the law of expectancy. In order to achieve a permanent success, even with hypnosis or by the renewing of your mind, the expectation must somehow become positive for lasting success; otherwise, even if a smoker sees the best hypnotherapist in the world, failure may devour the initial success. If he or she expects to backslide, it is only a matter of time before the expectation will be realized.

This is why many ministers start their sermons by having the audience or congregation begin to raise their expectations prior to the Word coming forth. Week in and week out, positive messages are sent forth and this is how the permanent success takes place, by raising our expectations to the level of our faith. If the minister or pastor does not raise this level, it's up to you to come into the service or sanctuary with high hopes that will match the level of your faith to give you the guaranteed results you're looking to receive for permanent change in your situation.

The brain and the nervous system respond only to mental images. It does not matter if the image is self-induced or from the external world; the mental image formed becomes the blueprint, and the subconscious mind uses every means at its disposal to carry out the plan. Worrying is a form of programming, a picture of what we don't want. But the subconscious mind acts to fulfill the pictured situation. **Job 3:25 — "Job said, 'For the thing which I greatly feared is come upon me, and that which I was afraid of is come unto me.'"** Job expected something bad to happen to him and it did, but with the grace and mercy of God Job's situation was turned around and he received twice as much as he had lost.

Many persons suffer from chronic anxiety, which is simply a subconscious mental expectancy that something terrible will happen. On the other hand, we all know people who seem to have the magic touch. Life seems to shower them with blessings for no apparent reason, and so we call them lucky. What seems to be luck is in reality *positive mental expectancy*, a strong belief that success is deserved. We become what we think about.

This is what faith is all about. Faith sees things before they take place and pushes us to accomplish those things which would have normally been impossible in our own minds or with our own strength. Faith propels us through the things in life that would usually become obstacles to our successes. When faith is present, **Philippians 4:13** says, **I can do all things through Christ which strengthen me.** We can do all things great and small. The Bible also gives us instruction that it is impossible to please God without this spiritual substance.

Physical health is largely dependent upon our mental expectancies. Physicians recognize that if a patient expects to remain sick, lame, paralyzed, and helpless, even to die, the expected condition tends to be realized. *Change the picture and change the results* – the expectancy of health, strength and well-being which then tends to be realized.

#3: Imagination is more powerful than knowledge when dealing with the mind.

Reason is easily overruled by imagination; this is why some persons blindly rush into some unreasonable act or situation. Violent crimes based upon jealousy are almost always caused by an over-active imagination. We can easily see that such people have allowed their imaginations to overcome reason. But we are often blind to our own superstitions, prejudices, and unreasonable beliefs. Ideas accompanied by a strong emotion such as anger, hatred, love or political and religious beliefs usually cannot be modified through the use of reason. This is also called the law of conflict, and when imagination and logic are in conflict, imagination usually wins.

I would like to state that in another way. If we try to make logical decisions by trying to bypass the route of our imagination, the attempt won't work.

Always remember that imagination is the language of the subconscious mind. I believe it is important to help people imagine total success, and I also suggest that they vividly remember the success that they have imagined, as the mind often responds to what we imagine. The issue is how do we manipulate the power of our imaginations and use it to our advantage. The Bible says that we should cast down every evil/wicked imagination and every high thing that exalts itself against the knowledge of God. So imagination in itself is not bad, as some would make it to be because of negative perceptions of things that have happened in the news.

The Bible often uses the word "rejoice." It's looking back at something that has happened in the past and remembering the victory, having joy all over again that what God has done in the past, He's more than able to do it all over again.

#4: Opposing ideas cannot be held at one and the same time.

This does not mean that two or more ideas cannot be remembered or harbored in your memory, but it refers to the conscious mind recognizing an idea. Many people try to hold opposing ideas simultaneously. A man might believe in honesty and expect his children to be honest, all while engaging daily in slightly dishonest business practices. He may try to justify this by saying, "All my competitors do it, it's an accepted practice." However, he cannot escape the conflict and its effect upon his nervous system that is caused by trying to hold opposing ideas within himself. I like to think of this as the conscience of a person. What makes you stick to your convictions or what you believe to be the right thing to do any difficult situations?

Paul stated it like this, in **Romans 7:15-17 — For that which I do I allow not: for what I would, that do**

I not; but what I hate, that do I. ¹⁶If then I do that which I would not, I consent unto the law that *it is* good. ¹⁷Now then it is no more I that do it, but sin that dwelleth in me.

This is one of the biggest reasons to know the word of God and to quote it when situations arise. You should be letting the Word dictate the proper response to your ideas to make sure that they are godly and not putting you in the predicament of being tossed to and fro, back and forth. **The Epistle of James** puts it this way in **Chapter 1:6: but let him ask in faith, nothing wavering. For he that wavereth is like a wave of the sea driven with the wind and tossed. Verse 7** says, **For let not that man think that he shall receive anything of the Lord.**

#5: **Once an idea has been accepted by the subconscious mind, it remains until it is replaced by another idea. The companion rule to this is the longer the idea remains, the more opposition there is to replacing it with a new idea.**

Once an idea has been accepted, it tends to remain in place. The longer it is held, the more it tends to become a fixed habit of thinking. This is how habits of action are formed, both good and bad. *First there is the thought and then the action.* We have habits of thinking as well as habits of action, but the thought or idea always comes first. Hence, it is obvious that if we want to change actions we must begin by changing thoughts. However, we have many thought habits which are not correct and yet are fixed in the mind. Some people believe that at critical times they must have a drink of vodka, a cigarette, a cup of coffee or a tranquilizer to steady their nerves so that they can perform effectively. This is not correct, but the idea is there, and is a fixed habit of thought. There will be opposition to replacing it with a correct idea.

We need to alter fixed ideas or learn to use them constructively. No matter how long they have remained they can be changed.

A child attacked by a vicious dog may get the idea that all dogs are dangerous. If that idea persists, then the phobia will become more sensitized every time a dog growls or barks at that child. Also, a person going up and down like a yo-yo with one diet after another can also become sensitized to the idea of failing at weight reduction; thus it becomes increasingly more difficult to believe in the ability ever to maintain control over his or her weight.

This is why reading God's word on a daily basis is so important to the Christian life. It's how those fixed thoughts are changed and replaced with more positive ones. It's how we can love in the midst of unloving people. It's how we can turn the other cheek when we're slapped. It's how we can smile in the face of adversity. It's how we can laugh when the bill collector continues to call.

I Corinthians 13:9 - 11 says, **For we know in part, and we prophesy in part** [10]**But when that which is perfect is come, then that which is in part shall be done away.** [11]**When I was a child, I spake as a child, I understood as a child, I thought as a child; but when I became a man, I put away childish things.**

Sometimes as Christians we just need to grow up. We know what we need to do and what is necessary to move forward to the next level in spiritual maturity, and we just need to stop making excuses, quit being lazy and be obedient to the voice of the Spirit of God and move.

#6: An emotionally induced symptom tends to cause organic change if persisted in long enough.

Many reputable medical men have acknowledged that more than 70% of human ailments are functional rather than organic. This means that the function of an organ or part of the body has been disturbed by the reaction of the nervous system to negative ideas held in the subconscious mind. *This is not meant to imply that every person who complains of an ailment is emotionally ill or neurotic.* There are diseases caused by germs, parasites, viruses, and other things attacking the human body. However, we are a mind in a body and the two cannot be separated. Therefore, if you continue to fear ill health, constantly talk about your "nervous stomach", high blood pressure", "sugar diabetes" or "tension headaches," in time organic changes must occur. **Proverbs 18:21 says, Death and life are in the power of the tongue: and they that love it shall eat the fruit thereof.**

You can actually change your symptoms with positive confessions. Start every day with a positive statement about yourself, even if it's the smallest thing you can think of, such as "I feel great." Each day, add a new confession and say it to yourself throughout the day. You'll start to push out those negative thoughts that have caused your system to react on the negative side and you'll begin to see a difference. What you are actually doing is stimulating your faith to believe. **Hebrews 11:3: Through faith we understand that the worlds were framed by the word of God, so that things which are seen were not made of things which do appear.** When you speak those things which were not seen, they will be seen in your life.

I'm reminded of a time when I had very little money and I began to confess that I would never be broke another day in my life. I made it a regular confession, and little by little money began to accumulate in my bank account and in my pocket.

Psychosomatic illness is a fact, and most of us realize that prolonged stress can have a negative impact on our health.

#7: Each suggestion acted upon creates less opposition to successive suggestion.

In other words, once a self-suggestion has been accepted by your subconscious mind, it becomes easier for additional suggestions to be accepted and acted upon.

Judges 16 tells the story of Samson and Delilah. Delilah badgered Samson. She wore him down until eventually he told her where his strength was. Each time Samson entertained her request, it created less opposition—not to mention that he lied to her with each answer.

¹⁶And it came to pass, when she pressed him daily with her words, and urged him, *so* that his soul was vexed unto death;

¹⁷That he told her all his heart, and said unto her, There hath not come a razor upon mine head; for I *have been* a Nazarite unto God from my mother's womb: if I be shaven, then my strength will go from me, and I shall become weak, and be like any *other* man.

¹⁸And when Delilah saw that he had told her all his heart, she sent and called for the lords of the Philistines, saying, Come up this once, for he hath shewed me all his heart. Then the lords of the

Philistines came up unto her, and brought money in their hand.

Here is another example in **Luke 18:1-5**:

And he spake a parable unto them to this end, that men ought always to pray, and not to faint;

² Saying, There was in a city a judge, which feared not God, neither regarded man:

³ And there was a widow in that city; and she came unto him, saying, Avenge me of mine adversary.

⁴ And he would not for a while: but afterward he said within himself, Though I fear not God, nor regard man;

⁵ Yet because this widow troubleth me, I will avenge her, lest by her continual coming she weary me.

The widow continued to pester the judge with each act of her visit to his chamber. He eventually gave in and granted her request to avenge her.

It's interesting that Jesus called reaction to such pressure "fainting."

#8: When dealing with the subconscious mind and its functions, the greater the conscious effort, the less the subconscious response.

This proves why willpower doesn't really exist! If you have insomnia you've learned the harder you try to go to sleep, the wider awake you become. The rule for dealing with the subconscious mind is to take it easy. You must work to develop a positive mental expectancy that your problem can be and will be solved. As your faith in your subconscious mind increases, you learn to let it happen rather than trying to force it to happen.

Hebrews 11:1; Now faith is the substance of things hoped for, the evidence of things not seen, verse 2; For by it the elders obtained a good report. This is faith. You have to believe it will happen and rest in the fact that it's done, without the proof. Utilize the substance or the stuff and just believe. Don't force it, believe; don't push, and just believe. It's like grace. You don't have to work for it, and you should not do anything but receive it. It's a gift from God.

The subconscious can be persuaded, but it cannot be forced without resistance.

Now let's look at the emotional side of the soul.

Chapter 2

* * *

Emotions

Did you know that emotions can alter the perceptions of real events? When we are in a state of emotion, we are propelled toward what we are imagining. In other words, emotion is the energy dynamo, or the motivating power of the mind.

Emotions have been described as a "universal language" because regardless of culture, we all experience emotions, positive or negative. It is most recognized with facial expression. Anywhere in the world you can see it in people's faces when they are happy, sad, disgusted, or surprised, but, this language can be read.

It is unknown as to how many emotions we can run through on a daily basis, but I believe that the range of emotions can be controlled. Some people use music or other arts to help control their emotions. When you come home from a hard day at work, you might choose to play some music to help change your mood or shift the emotional balance of what transpired earlier in the day. There's something about hearing a favorite song and the joy it can bring. Emotions tend to come and go.

If two emotions exist at the same time, the dominant one wins out over the weaker one, such as in the example of a ball player wanting to hit a home run, but striking out because of his more powerful fear of doing so. Caught in the fear, if he imagines striking out he is more prone to doing just that as the idea of missing the ball is emotionally energized right into the mind.

We cannot give into fear at any time. Fear has been defined by some as False Evidence Appearing Real (FEAR). We as Christians have to operate with faith. The Bible is very clear in **Hebrews 11: 6: But without faith it is impossible to please him; for he that cometh to God must believe that he is, and that he is a rewarded of them that diligently seek him**. Walking by faith and not by sight (**II Corinthians 5:7**) will help us eliminate the issues associated with being led by our emotional makeup.

I talked about triggers earlier and what makes us respond to certain outside influences. The sooner we can recognize what our "hot buttons" are or our "emotional triggers" and what makes us respond to these influences, the better we will become at controlling our emotional highs and lows. We could be reacting to things that were planted by our parents, peers or others when we were very young.

Basic Definitions

- Emotion: any specific feeling; any of various complex reactions with both mental and physical manifestations, as love, hate, fear, anger
- Ambivalence: simultaneous conflicting feelings toward a person or thing, as love and hate
- Apathy: lack of emotion; lack of interest, indifference (just don't care)

Next, you will see a list of specific emotions that we may process throughout the day.

Specific Emotions

- Agape: spontaneous, altruistic love
- Amusement: entertained, laughing, smiling; pleasantly or enjoyably occupied or interested
- Anger: a feeling of displeasure resulting from injury, mistreatment, or opposition and usually showing itself in a desire to fight back at the supposed cause of this feeling. Anger is an emotion related to one's psychological interpretation of having been offended, wronged, or denied, and a tendency to react through retaliation. Anger is a symptom, a way of cloaking and express feelings too awful to experience directly—hurt, bitterness, grief, and most of all, fear.

- <u>Bored</u>: to be weary by being dull, uninteresting, or monotonous
- <u>Comfortable</u>: a state of ease and quiet enjoyment, free from worry, pain, etc.
- <u>Courage</u>: the attitude of facing and dealing with anything recognized as dangerous, difficult or painful instead of withdrawing from it; the quality of being fearless or brave
- <u>Cowardice</u>: shamefully excessive fear of danger, difficulty, or suffering
- <u>Embarrassed</u>: to feel self-conscious, confused and ill at ease
- <u>Envy</u>: desire for some advantage, quality, etc. that another has; a feeling of discontent and ill because of another's advantages, possessions, etc.
- <u>Excited</u>: emotionally aroused
- <u>Fear</u>: a feeling of anxiety and agitation caused by the presence or nearness of danger, evil, pain, etc.; a feeling of uneasiness or apprehension. Fear may be the first enemy you face in our society. It is the most destructive emotion there is. Cold feet, panic, depression and violence are all symptoms of fear when it's out of control. But this feeling, ironically, can also trigger courage, alertness, and objectivity. You must not to try to rid yourself of this basic human emotion, but instead learn to manipulate it to your own advantage. You cannot surrender to fear, but you can use it as a kind of fuel.

- <u>Foolish</u>: silly, ridiculous, embarrassed
- <u>Gratitude</u>: a feeling of thankful appreciation for favors or benefits received; thankfulness
- <u>Happy</u>: a feeling of great pleasure, contentment, joy
- <u>Heartache</u>: sorrow or grief; mental anguish
- <u>Heartbroken</u>: overwhelmed with sorrow, grief or disappointment
- <u>Heartsick</u>: extremely unhappy or despondent
- <u>Honor</u>: high regard or great respect
- <u>Hope</u>: a feeling that what is wanted will happen; desire accompanied by expectation
- <u>Hopeless</u>: without hope; despair
- <u>Humility</u>: absence of pride or self-assertion
- <u>Jealous</u>: resentfully suspicious of a rival or a rival's influence
- <u>Love</u>: a deep or tender feeling of affections for or attachment or devotion to a person
- <u>Modesty</u>: having a moderate opinion of one's own value
- <u>Paranoia</u>: delusions of persecution; over-suspiciousness
- <u>Pride</u>: respect for oneself, sense of one's own worth, self-respect
- <u>Regret</u>: to feel troubled or remorseful over one's own acts
- <u>Relief</u>: an easing, as of pain, discomfort or anxiety; a lightening of a burden
- <u>Respect</u>: hold in high regard; feel esteem for; to consider or treat with deference or dutiful regard

- <u>Sad</u>: having low spirits or sorrow; unhappy, mournful
- <u>Shame</u>: a painful feeling of having lost the respect of others because of the improper behavior, incompetence, etc. of oneself or another
- <u>Vain</u>: having or showing an excessively high regard for one's self, looks, possessions, abilities

As you can see, the list can be pretty exhaustive especially when we may not in total control of our emotions. Up one minute and down the next.

Out of such a list of emotions, the Bible is clear that there is one emotion that is greater than them all.

In I Corinthians 13:13 it reads, "And now abideth faith, hope and charity, these three but the greatest of these is charity". Love here has been translated as charity, but it is evident that the greatest of these is love.

Survival

Our emotions have the potential to serve us today as a delicate and sophisticated internal guidance system. Our emotions alert us when natural human needs are not being met. For example, when we feel lonely, our need for connection with other people is unmet. When we feel afraid, our need for safety is unmet. When we feel rejected, it is our need for acceptance which is unmet.

Decision Making

Our emotions help us make decisions. Studies show that when a person's emotional connections are severed in the brain, he cannot make even simple decisions. Why? Because he doesn't know how he will *feel* about his choices.

Boundary Setting

When we feel uncomfortable with a person's behavior, our emotions alert us. If we learn to trust our emotions and feel confident expressing ourselves, we can let the person know we feel uncomfortable as soon as we are aware of our feeling. Some people have called that having some "personal space".

Communication

Our emotions help us communicate with others. Our facial expressions, for example, can convey a wide range of emotions. If we look sad or hurt, we are signaling to others that we need their help. If we are verbally skilled we will be able to express more of our emotional needs and thereby have a better chance of filling them. If we are effective at listening to the emotional troubles of others, we are better able to help them feel understood, important and cared about.

Unity

Our emotions are perhaps the greatest potential source of uniting all members of the human species. Clearly, our various religious, cultural and political beliefs have not united us. Far too often, in fact, they have tragically and even fatally divided us. Emotions, on the other hand, are universal.

Emotional Intelligence

I would like to introduce a new subject that some may have never heard of, and that's Emotional Intelligence (EI). This refers to the ability to perceive, control and evaluate emotions. Since 1990, psychologists Peter Salovey and John D. Mayer have been the leading researchers on emotional intelligence. In their influential article titled "Emotional

Intelligence," they defined emotional intelligence as "the subset of social intelligence that involves the ability to monitor one's own and others' feelings and emotions, to discriminate among them and to use this information to guide one's thinking and actions" (1990).

This definition was amended in 2007 to include an emphasis on emotional intelligence as an innate potential:

Emotional intelligence is the innate potential to feel, use, communicate, recognize, remember, describe, identify, learn from, manage, understand and explain emotions. (S. Hein, 2007)

Salovey and Mayer proposed a model that identified four different factors of emotional intelligence:

1. **Perceiving Emotions:** The first step in understanding emotions is to accurately perceive them. In many cases, this might involve understanding nonverbal signals such as body language and facial expressions.

2. **Reasoning with Emotions:** The next step involves using emotions to promote thinking and cognitive activity. Emotions help prioritize what we pay attention to and react to; we respond emotionally to things that garner our attention.

3. **Understanding Emotions:** The emotions that we perceive can carry a wide variety of meanings. If someone is expressing angry emotions, the observer must interpret the cause of their anger and what it might mean. For example, if your boss is acting angry, it might mean that he or she is dissatisfied with your work, or it could be that he got a speeding ticket on his way to work that morning, or that he's been fighting with his wife.

4. **Managing Emotions:** The ability to manage emotions effectively is a key part of emotional intelligence. Regulating emotions, responding appropriately, and responding to the emotions of others are all important aspects of emotional intelligence.

Chapter 3

* * *

Finally, the Will

I would like to start off with the definition of a decision since this is what the input from the mind and emotions will pour into.

It has been said or proven that men make decision based on information, facts or intellect, while women make these based on emotion. So you see that both inputs may and should be necessary.

The definition of a decision:

1. The act or process of deciding; determination, as of a question or doubt, by making a judgment. *They must make a decision between these two contestants.*
2. The act of or need for making up one's mind. *This is a difficult decision.*
3. Something that is decided; resolution. *He made a poor decision.*
4. A judgment, as one formally pronounced by a court.

5. The quality of being decided; firmness: *He spoke with decision.*

Wikipedia puts it this way: A decision is the selection between possible <u>actions</u>, while a choice is the selection between two or more <u>objects</u>.

Decision making can be regarded as the mental (or cognitive) process resulting in the selection of a course of action among several alternative scenarios. Every decision making process produces a final choice. The output can be an action or an opinion of a choice.

What happened in the Garden of Gethsemane was the ultimate act of making up one's mind. Jesus was agonizing over making the right decision. He was faced with two possible actions, being beaten and wounded and then going to the cross or not going to endure the pain, hardship and crucifixion. It was so tough that drops of blood came down from his brow. Let's follow along with the book of **Mark 14**:

³² And they came to a place which was named Gethsemane: and he saith to his disciples, Sit ye here, while I shall pray.

³³ And he taketh with him Peter and James and John, and began to be sore amazed, and to be very heavy;

³⁴ And saith unto them, My soul is exceeding sorrowful unto death: tarry ye here, and watch.

³⁵ And he went forward a little, and fell on the ground, and prayed that, if it were possible, the hour might pass from him.

³⁶ And he said, Abba, Father, all things are possible unto thee; take away this cup from me: nevertheless not what I will, but what thou wilt.

Our decisions should be based on what God wants for our lives and not always what we want. We should be pushing ourselves on a daily basis to say and make decisions that are truly not about us.

I like the saying "Love looks to give, and lust looks to take." We have to posture ourselves so that our lives are giving and our decisions to do so are not agonizing.

The key word in most of the definitions listed above is *action*. When a decision is made, some type of action will follow. We are the sum total of every decision that has been made in the past, some good and some bad. We've all made choices that got us to this point. I'm writing this book to help us get out of the situations where we are continually making bad decisions and ultimately setting up ourselves, and possibly our families, to fail. That is not God's best for our lives.

We have to take good information from godly sources and record over those bad tapes that have driving us for years. This process of renewing the mind is the ultimate challenge of being a Christian. I like the definition "The act of or need for making up one's mind," which takes us back to the point where we see that in us reside two distinct points of view, minds, or opinions. As these "new creatures which have never existed before," we have to always be conscious that we must choose the right path, or act on the correct choice that will keep us in the perfect will of God.

When Jesus went to the cross to redeem us back to the Father, he saved us from hell, not from trouble. The Bible tells us in **Psalm 34:19: Many are the afflictions of the righteous: but the Lord delivereth him out of them all**. I believe that some, if not most, of these afflictions can be avoided if we make better decisions. Better decisions create better actions which cause us to be better husbands, fathers, workers, friends, etc.

CONCLUSION

Joshua 1:8 says, **This book of the law shall not depart out of thy mouth; but thou shalt meditate therein day and night, that thou mayest observe to do according to all that is written therein: for then thou shalt make thy way prosperous, and then thou shalt have good success.**

Psalm 19:14 says, **Let the words of my mouth, and the meditation of my heart, be acceptable in thy sight, O LORD, my strength, and my redeemer.**

I started out talking about how we have a tendency to play "old tapes" from things that have been recorded in our past, and how these tapes have been accepted without thinking about them. We have now received information about how to deal with the influence of these tapes, and how to remove the triggers.

In order to live victoriously as Christians, we need to make certain changes and adjustments in the way we think, act and respond to the challenges we are faced with each and every day. These adjustments can and will make the difference in you moving forward or becoming stagnated in your growth and walk with the Lord.

As we make the commitment to renew our minds on a daily basis, we will continue to mature and develop into the strong individuals we were chosen to be. We will have a positive impact in our communities, on our jobs, in school, and wherever we are. We will be the type of person that people will look up to as role models for their own lives. This is not saying that we will live "perfect" lives, but that we will be moving in the direction where less is seen of us, and more is seen of the Christ in us. The character of God will be more visible and people will be able to distinguish that we are Christians, and that our light is not just a flicker but shines so brightly that we won't be able to hide it under a bushel but will let others see so that they can be attracted to it.

Luke 11:33 says, **No man, when he hath lighted a candle, putteth it in a secret place, neither under a bushel, but on a candlestick, that they which come in may see the light.**

REFERENCES

Excerpts taken from the book titled, *The Art of Hypnosis: Mr. Charles Tebbetts Hypnotism Training Course* by C. Roy Hunter. "Rules of the Mind" were taken from Chapter 11 on concepts about the subconscious.

Some information was taken from Kendra Cherry, About.com Guide and can also be found at psychology.about.com under personality development.

ABOUT THE AUTHOR

Edward J. Lee was born in Washington, DC and was raised in the suburbs of the metropolitan area in the small town of Glenarden, Maryland. He currently resides in Prince George's County, Maryland, and has raised two wonderful sons, Justin and Joshua Lee. He is a member of Victory Christian Ministries International where he has drawn his inspiration to write this book in order to help others overcome issues of life.

Made in the USA
Middletown, DE
02 July 2021